I.C.U.

The Comprehensive Guide to Breathing Life Back Into Your Personal Brand

SHEILA A. ANDERSON

ROGUE
cre·a·tive

For ordering information or special discounts for
bulk purchases, please contact:

Image Power Play
1500 North Tahoe Trail, Sioux Falls, SD 57110
(605) 310-7166   sheila@ImagePowerPlay.com

Cover Design/Illustration and composition
by Brad Szollose of Rogue Creative.

Cover Photo Credit: Chad Phillips Photography

Cataloging-in-Publication data
ISBN 13: 978-0-692-98043-9

First Edition

WHAT PEOPLE ARE
SAYING ABOUT I.C.U.

66 You only get one shot to make a 1st impression. By reading Sheila Anderson's book, you'll have them at 'hello!'"

Jeffrey W. Hayzlett
Primetime TV & Radio Host,
Speaker, Author and Part-Time Cowboy

66 No one who ever made a significant difference did so by following the rules! Sheila Anderson gives you permission to break the rules that stifle the expression of you as a brand."

Dov Baron
Inc.com Top 100 Leadership Speaker,
Consultant and Bestselling Author
www.FullMontyLeadership.com

66 Sheila Anderson is a knowledgeable and talented expert on personal branding. She has an innate understanding and the experience and training to back up her expertise. Sheila certified as a Universal Style consultant and received advanced training in the Universal Style System which unites inner essence with outer expression. This is the very heart of personal branding, and her new book I.C.U., Breathing Life Back Into Your Personal Brand

provides a clear path to achieving this successful, powerful identifier."

Alyce Parsons, AICI, CIP, CET, CIHM
Author of StyleSource and five textbooks
on style used by FIT since 1990.
International trainer, speaker and founder
of AICI (Association of Image Consultants International)

❝❝ As air is to humans, so is Sheila A. Anderson's Book I.C.U., Breathing Life Back into Your Personal Brand."

Pat McGill
Speaker/Author

❝❝ Brand matters. Always. To be successful you need a new plan and a new understanding of what Brand means now. This book is that roadmap."

Janet Schijns
Go to Market Expert

❝❝ While some people talk about personal branding, Sheila Anderson does a great job of guiding you through this important process in professional growth. There are several books on the market that speak to personal branding, but none offer the reader the insight and thoughtfulness on this topic like the I.C.U., Breathing Life Back into Your Personal Brand book. Sheila shares the important steps that she has perfected with years of experience and brings it to you in a way in which everyone can benefit."

Michael P. Williams
Chief Marketing Officer
Sports marketing and digital marketing expert

❝ Personal Branding is critical in today's visual world. Your personal brand will make or break your business. Sheila A. Anderson brings personal style, elegance and fun back into your daily routine. I highly recommend this book to anyone looking to up their game. Lastly... Sheila A. Anderson walks her talk... What a fabulous personal brand."

Lea Woodford
CEO SmartFem Media Group and SmartFem TV Host

❝ Your brand and image define how others perceive you, there is no denying that! What I love most about Sheila, is she makes it easy to take a topic that can seem overwhelming to change or influence and gives you practical tools to start shifting to live the brand and image you desire. She has spent time in front of many of my clients, and everyone walks away with valuable tools to implement. Breathe life into your personal brand by taking part in this book. Thank you Sheila for taking the time to create this "How To!"

Dina B. Simon
CEO of Simon Says Lead
Author, Executive Coach and Board Chair

❝ I.C.U. gives you the permission and knowledge to take ownership, embracing all that you are. Building a stage and having the courage to live out your personal brand where you and your audience take the plaudits for the way you lead yourself and those around you."

Mark Sephton
Mentor to entrepreneurs
Author, contributor for **entrepreneur.com**
Radio Show host of "Talk Business"
Radio Plus Coventry and international speaker

THANK YOU

Special Thanks goes out to Julie Ann Sullivan and Kathleen Caldwell, my Publishing Divas, who stood by me and guided me through every step of writing this book. It has been an experience I will truly treasure. Your gift of friendship has touched my life forever.

My husband and best friend, Derry Anderson for **not stifling me** and giving me a beautiful life filled with love and joy. Thank you for embracing all my ideas and encouraging me to pursue my deepest passions.

Jeffrey W. Hayzlett whose boldness challenges me every day to think big. Your drive and energy spur me to work relentlessly and fosters confidence in my ability to make an impact in this world. My relationship with you and the entire C-Suite Network team have yielded tremendous professional opportunities and personal fulfillment. I continue to be awed.

Lindsey Hayzlett for your continuous support and contribution to this project. You are my twin in many ways!

Sylvie di Giusto for your guidance, inspiration, and belief. I will always be grateful to you for pushing me to be my best self and all you have brought into my life.

My mother, Colette; my father, Richard; and brother, Todd, for your love and support in letting me be me.

Kathy Sazama, I consider you the sister I never had! You have been with me from the very beginning of my style and image journey. You have been my rock in endless ways.

Chad Phillips for your discerning eye in capturing my true essence. I am proud to display your photography on the cover.

Michelle LeBow and Julia Green for your brilliant editorial help.

Light Artist Photography and John and Kathy Krysak for the unique vintage photoshoot.

Brad Szollose for helping me dig deep into my soul. Thank you for guiding me personally and professionally. Your gift of creativity and design shines on the book cover and layout.

CONTENTS

FOREWORD

Image is not just what you wear; it is how you communicate yourself to the outside world in all aspects. It can
be an overwhelming process and a difficult task to begin
with, but it doesn't have to be. The I.C.U. Rule: Breathing
Life Back Into Your Personal Brand, helps guide readers
through the necessary steps to create their own
personal image.

The idea of creating a personal brand is often intimidat-
ing. Where do you begin? When do we know it's time for
a change? Sheila A. Anderson is someone who thrives on
inspiring others to make the necessary changes to polish
their image. Her book guides you through everything you
need to know with ease. Through personal anecdotes,
worksheets, and she asks poignant questions to make you
delve deeper into yourself for the answers you need.

Sheila teaches you that you can be unforgettable, too. If
there's anything I've learned in this business, it's that you
want people to know who you are. Sheila helps you figure
out your personal brand by identifying, as she defines it,
your "inner persona," and finding ways to communicate

that to the outside world.

Through my work, I had the chance to meet Sheila, and she is now a great friend of many years. You never miss her when she walks into a room. With her unique style and strong, yet warm presence, she's also hard to forget. Everything she wears is meticulously calculated and intentional. When it comes to the I.C.U. method, Sheila doesn't just talk the talk: she walks the walk. Once you meet her, you don't forget her.

As the General Manager of the C-Suite Network (which includes TV, Radio, Advisors and multiple business networking events), I have to maintain an image that is consistent, but still reflective of who I am. Following the I.C.U. method, I created an image that people recognize: professional yet approachable, and always styled to a T.

Sheila prides herself on her unforgettable trademark ROI, or 'Return On Image.' This book helps coach your own Return On Image. By creating a personal brand, you increase your value as an asset to your company and to others.

So what is the ICU Method, anyway?

"I": Intentional

What are your goals? What are your values and strengths? What qualities/words do you feel describe you? Do these match how others see you? Sheila walks you through answering these questions for yourself.

"C": Consistent

Your image doesn't take a vacation. It maintains through all aspects of your life: through in-person interactions, your social media pages, even your outgoing voicemail. Keeping all your assets consistent helps you create a personal brand that's unmatched.

Just look through all of Sheila's social platforms: Linke-dIn, Twitter, Instagram. There's no question that the same person is behind all of these pages. Find a signature that helps you define your look, and remember – your image is your logo (Sheila, for example, has a knack for statement eyewear and jewelry)!

"U": You

Apply what you've figured out to your life. Gain visibility in your community, and show off your brand and how it adds value to said community. Improve your strengths and network by volunteering. If you work for a corporate brand, influence it and grow yourself through speaking events, networking opportunities, and by creating content. Figure out all the ways you communicate and implement your personal brand on all of those.

Remember these steps, find your personal brand, embody it in every way possible, and become unforgettable. You only have one chance to make a good first impression!

C-SUITE NETWORK ™

Lindsey Hayzlett
General Manager of Thought Leadership
at the **C-Suite Network**
Host of **Your Legacy**

x

INTRODUCTION

Everything communicates.
It's as simple as that.
It's as complex as that.

Personal Branding...

It's about alignment; the proper positioning of who you are at your very core that exudes through every touch point with you as a human.

It's about owning the experience every person has with you and what he or she remembers or says about you when you are not in their presence.

It's about bringing forward your values and strengths and sowing them into the lives of others for the better in a way that no one else can.

It's about being intentional, being consistent, and being you.

It's about never sacrificing your individuality when others think you should be someone else.

It's about standing firm on your beliefs.
It's about a polished outward appearance
 that exemplifies **your internal persona.**
It's about positioning yourself.
It's about being strategically visible.

Don't Stifle Me

I have worked my whole life for my image to reflect who I truly am in my heart. Social rules surround us, rules for this and rules for that. I am creative by nature – creative is who I am and who I will always be. I don't like rules much. In fact, I feel stifled by rules.

With an artistic flair from a very early age, I have a keen eye for how things look. I didn't realize it at the time, but my artistic flair and view of the world is really why I am all about first impressions and personal image.

As a child, my personal space was just a tiny bedroom, but my room was already a reflection of me. I remember being so excited when I got to choose graphic wallpaper for my bedroom walls and was also able to pick out a coordinating paint color. In fact, I didn't just select one wallpaper design, I picked out two patterns that coordinated. This was back in the 70s when earth tones were all the rage. However, I did not want to do brown. I wanted something with a punch! I was drawn to the vibrancy of the color orange, so that's what I chose: an orange and brown square patterned wallpaper with a large pattern and a similar one with a smaller pattern. I instinctively knew I had to vary the scale so they went together. I selected an orange paint for the other two walls. Of course, I had to get new window coverings and bedspread to match. I was in all my glory! I loved being in my room and admiring how it all went together. The details of accessories and their placement throughout my bedroom were purposely placed. I did not know all the interior design rules. I simply had an eye for it and knew when it looked right. I even did this to end tables around the house to make sure the object was in the best position possible that brought attention to it... showed it in the best light. I brought my friends over after school and beamed with joy at their reaction when they first entered my room. As just a young girl, my friends' first impression of my room thrilled me.

> As just a young girl, my friends' first impression of my room thrilled me.

I moved from creating my own personal oasis in my bedroom into helping my mom. I remember one evening; my mom and dad had the neighbors over for dinner. My mom was busy making deviled eggs, and I grabbed the carpet rake to fluff the shag rug in the foyer before the guests arrived. I'd step back and admire my work. I loved how the carpet's matted footmarks disappeared and the shag fibers leaned neatly in alignment. Crazy, I know. But again, I was tuned into how things first appeared.

To this day, I am still in tune with first appearances. I've moved on from raking shag carpets; when I enter office buildings or clinics, I fluff the leaves on the silk plants. My husband shakes his head, but I can't help myself. It's who I am to my very core. In fact, I almost became an interior designer. Again, both professions are about first impressions. So it makes complete sense that I found my passion in image consulting. I like to say, "I decorate people!"

When I first explored my own style and image, I learned by trial and error. I felt trapped by what I thought society wanted me to be. I often wondered, "Why did there have to be so many rules for how people should look?" Everyone looked bland to me, like a cookie cutter. I felt like I was in a brown box, and I wanted to be in a striking foil wrapped box topped with a luscious bow -- inviting you to open it and find the amazing gift inside.

As I explored my style, there were many times my husband gave me that look. You know the one, the one that says, **"Do you really think that's a good idea to wear that?"** Thankfully my best friend, Kathy, who later became my business partner, told me **"Don't let him stifle you."**

And so as my life's journey as an image expert began, I decided I wasn't going to let enyone or anything stifle me.

And so my life's journey as an image expert began. I decided I wasn't going to let anyone or anything stifle me. I had a new-found confidence. I gave myself permission to be myself.

Now I'd like to tell you from here on out I was perfect right away– that it was easy for me to be myself, and it was a snap for me to figure out my style. The fact is, that is far from reality. And, yet when my husband gives me that look, I say -- with a sly grin, **"Honey, don't stifle me!"**

Now, right around this time, my husband was figuring out his personal brand, finding his own authentic style. He was new in the corporate world, and as a Certified Public

Accountant ... well, I imagine you just had an image pop into your head of what you think an accountant looks like. Let me guess, a very basic suit, likely not highly expensive. If even a suit, maybe a sport coat with khaki dress pants, simple necktie, collared shirt, and plain oxford shoes. Am I close?

Surprise! My husband isn't a typical accountant. He, too, has a creative side. I've found you can be creative with numbers to some extent, but he wanted to express his creativity in a way other than with a calculator. He started wearing bolder patterns. In his work attire, he expressed his individuality with neckwear. In his casual attire, he often chose unique patterned shirts. The tables turned a bit and I gave HIM "the look." And he'd say to me ... you guessed it, "Honey, don't stifle me!" Our secret joke.

So why do I tell you all of this? The answer is simple. When it comes to your personal brand and image, my rule is bending the rules! Make the rules fit you! Don't let the rules stifle you!

In the following pages, I'm excited to share with you the **I.C.U. Rule™** and the process I have developed to breathing life back into your personal brand:

"I": Intentional
Be intentional before encounters even occur.
"C": Consistent
Be consistent in every way you present yourself.
"U": You
Be authentic to who you are and solidify the brand experience by prioritizing "you" or relationships, audiences, and communities.

I.C.U. is the way I work with leaders to lean into personal style and build an authentic brand. In this book, I'll share with you my three simple anchors I use to coach executives and business leaders on authentic style as it relates to personal brand. This three step I.C.U. formula changes the way leaders build their signature brand and achieve a **Return on Image®.**

 The I.C.U. Rule™ will help you own who you are. The end result is a lively personal brand that engages others and makes you memorable. You will become visible. Others will take notice and say, "I see you."

SECTION I
I – INTENTIONAL

"

in·ten·tion·al

adjective: done on purpose;
deliberate.

.

DEFINE YOURSELF BEFORE OTHERS DEFINE YOU.

"Accept no one's definition
of your life. Define yourself."
- Robert Frost

The first step focuses on being intentional before encounters occur. **Being intentional teaches people how to have a relationship with you.**

In many ways personal branding is the same as defining and building a corporate brand. Similarly, the very first step for each is to define who you are and what you stand for. So let's begin.

Don't leave your brand to chance.

If you haven't thought about the way you come across within the first several seconds of meeting people, don't worry … they've already done it for you. We all judge people whether we like to admit it or not. This is human nature.

1

The reality is, judgment happens every day, and really, in every moment. Various studies out there claim that as humans the average person interacts with about 80,000 people in their lifetime or meets 20,000 – 50,000 people. There are many variables involved. The point is not the exact number. The point is, it is important to understand the concept of the thousands of people we meet in our lifetime and the thousands of impressions we have made with these people. The goal of this concept is for your impressions to be memorable.

Do you have curb appeal?

Similar to when you drive by a house or walk by a brownstone, you judge it. You decide if the dwelling is even something you want to look at further or explore inside. The structure has to have curb appeal that is inviting. **First of all, is the overall style attractive to you?** Is the exterior finish color appealing and well maintained? Next, if the home has a yard, is the lawn a lush green carpet that makes you want to toss off your shoes and run through it barefoot? Or maybe there is no grass and the rocks and mulch are free from any weeds and placed in a design that is visually appealing. Or maybe it is simply the front door to the home or building that draws you in. Is it kept clean and free from litter? Is the sidewalk or porch swept? Is the landscaping manicured to perfection? Are there decorative elements to the home or building that add interest such as corbels, shutters, window boxes, high peaks, or fencing? **The outside must appeal to you in order for you to decide if you want to see more.** This same thought process applies to you personally. Think about this: do you have curb appeal?

No one is **you** and
that is your power.

Have you thought about:
- · How you want people to experience you?
- · What is your power?
- · Is your outside presence in harmony
  with who you are internally?
- · How people interpret you?

It is time to get honest with who you are and what presence you want to command. The following exercises are meant to help guide you through the process of defining yourself. This will take you some time to complete and you may not get the following questions all done in one setting. In fact, I suggest you find a quiet space – whether that be in your office, on the porch, or somewhere out in nature – or even do some meditation beforehand – to help you get into the reflection zone.

Goals

Noun: the object of a person's ambition or effort; an aim or desired result.

The very first thing you need to define is what your overall goals are for you personally and in business. What is it that you want to achieve and what does that success look like to you? There is a reason you are reading this book and have an interest in personal branding. You want to be sure you are getting the desired outcome you are striving for, and you know that having a solid personal brand can help you achieve this. One's personal brand is tied directly to the goals of an individual. Your goals will be a guiding force in determining how you will show up in every interaction with others.

What is it that you want to be recognized for as an individual?

_____
_____
_____
_____
_____
_____

What is that you want to be recognized for in your field?

_____
_____
_____
_____
_____
_____

The Words You Own

Circle 10 words that you feel best describe you. If there are other words not on this list that you feel represent you, please write those in using the blanks at the end of the list.

Adaptable
Affectionate
Amicable
Analytical
Artistic
Athletic
Bold
Carefree
Cautious
Charismatic
Charming
Conservative
Considerate
Controlled
Courageous
Creative
Decisive
Dependable
Detailed
Direct
Dramatic
Driven
Economical
Edgy
Elegant
Emotional
Empathetic
Energetic

Faithful

Feisty

Friendly

Fun

Graceful

Grateful

Happy

Harmonious

Honest

Humorous

Impulsive

Independent

Industrious

Intelligent

Kind

Loving

Magnetic

Mindful

Nice

Obsessive

Opinionated

Organized

Outgoing

Passionate

Perky

Persistent

Playful

Pleasant

Positive

Professional

Quiet

Refined

Reserved

Risk-taker

Romantic

Sarcastic

Sensible

Shy

Sweet

Sympathetic

Tenacious

Thoughtful

Tidy

Traditional

Truthful

Vivacious

Unique

Wise

Witty

Zestful

1. _____

2. _____

3. _____

4. _____

5. _____

6. _____

7. _____

8. _____

9. _____

10. _____

Narrow this list down to just 5 words:

- _____
- _____
- _____
- _____
- _____

Think about why you eliminated the 5 words and write down your thoughts on why they did not make the cut.

_____
_____
_____
_____
_____
_____

Now, narrow down these 5 words to just 3.

- _____
- _____
- _____

Are these the 3 words you want to own in the mind of others when they think of you?

_____
_____
_____
_____
_____
_____

Why do these 3 words best describe you?

_____

_____

_____

_____

_____

_____

Most recently how did you demonstrate these?

_____

_____

_____

_____

_____

_____

How are you living these 3 words?

_____

_____

_____

_____

_____

_____

Now, narrow down these 3 words to just 1.

What word feels right and in alignment with who you
are and what you want to own in the minds of others?

MY BRAND WORD IS:

_____

The brand word you choose will attach a personality, an attitude if you will, to your brand.

Values

Noun: A person's principles or standards of behavior; one's judgment of what is important in life.

Let's now define your values. First of all, why do they even matter? Values help guide you in situations where you need to decide right from wrong when things may not be clear. This will help you make better choices and decisions, and helps define who you are.

To get you thinking, answer these questions:

Was there a time you had to make a decision that wasn't a popular one? What guided you in that decision-making process?

_____
_____
_____
_____
_____
_____

What frustrates or upsets you? Why?

_____
_____
_____
_____
_____
_____

Do you have any deeply rooted family values?

_____
_____
_____
_____
_____
_____

What do you find attractive in the people you look up to?

_____
_____
_____
_____
_____
_____

Now, begin to list out your values and why they are important to you. There is not a magic number for how many you have, but I like people to stay at 10 or under. Because values are so unique to each individual, I am not going to provide a list to choose from.

VALUE	WHY THIS IS IMPORTANT TO ME
1.	
2.	
3.	
4.	
5.	
6.	
7.	
8.	
9.	
10.	

Strengths

Noun: a strong attribute.

Now it is time to think about what you do best. We tend to be able to list a litany of things we are not good at, but how often do you think about the things you do well? What do others compliment you on? What do you find easy to do that others might find challenging?

Most unhappiness comes from comparison. We look at others and want to be able to do what they do with the same ease and effort, but for us it is not our gift ... not our strength. I'm no different from you. Listing my strengths was a challenge.

One of the books that helped me most when I was searching for my strengths is **StrengthsFinder.** There is an online assessment you take to discover your natural talents. According to the website **www.strengths.gallup,** this book and assessment tool "... **will change the way you look at yourself -- and the world around you -- forever."** I strongly encourage you get the book. The main idea is for you to focus all of your energy on your strengths -- the things you are naturally gifted with -- and forget about trying to im-prove upon the things you are not good at. Why waste the energy? I agree wholeheartedly with this. **If you are going to exert energy into something, it might as well be on things you are good at.**

If you have not read this book or taken the assessment, here are some questions to answer as you think about your strengths:

What do I do best?

_____
_____
_____

What do others compliment me on?

_____
_____
_____
_____
_____
_____

What do I find easy that others ask me to do for them or help them with?

_____
_____
_____
_____
_____

I am most happy when doing this.

_____
_____
_____
_____
_____

I am proud of this.

_____

_____

_____

_____

_____

My strengths are:

- _____
- _____
- _____
- _____
- _____

I am.

We have all said this: "she has a great personality." But have you thought about yours? **Your personality draws people into you.** There are numerous personality tests out there, but the ones I find most fascinating are those that ask you questions on how you think of yourself in terms of how you relate to other things. This helps you further define your brand's persona. Your personality, or your brand's persona, creates a connection that speaks to others. **A brand persona is a collection human-like characteristics such as traits, attitudes, values, and strengths to which others can relate.**

This or That?

Compare the two words and circle which one fits you best and your brand characteristics. Think in terms of who you are and also who you want to be.

Detailed	Inexact
Formal	Casual
Progressive	Conservative
Sedan	SUV
Extravagant	Economical
Creative	Sporty
Elegant	Trendy
Loud	Silent
Serious	Carefree
Old	Young
Energetic	Laidback
Big	Small
Caregiver	Dependent
Understanding	Unrelenting

Associations to the words above should be in alignment to your personal brand. These words help paint the picture of how you view yourself.

Check Your BP (Brand Pulse)

Now that you have looked internally to who you want to be and the image and personal brand you want to pro-claim, it is time to assess how others perceive you. This is often a hard thing to do because of the vulnerability it can entail. I am not going to lie to you, there are times the results are hard to swallow. In our own minds, we very likely feel we are doing a superb job at showing the world who we are. You have to think in terms that everyone you come in contact with has formed some opinion of you based on the interaction. This interaction can be as simple as a phone conversation or as complex as a person who has known you most of your life. You will want to get feedback from a variety of people who have had different interactions with you. The results will help you figure out the areas that need some adjustments.

This **BP** check helps you determine if the perceived view fits the perception you want to own in the minds of others.

  This BP check helps you determine if the perceived view fits the perception you want to own in the minds of others.

  It's important to know how others currently perceive you. Having this insight will help you determine if the image you are portraying is in line with what you want it to be or if there are changes you need to make to get it in line.

Google yourself and write down what you find.

Look at what shows up in the feed and also click on the images tab.

_____

_____

_____

_____

_____

Look at your social media accounts and see where there is consistency and note any inconsistencies:

- Profile Photo
- Header Info
- Bio
- Email Address
- Completed Profiles
- Voice Tone

Ask 10 people – these can be friends, relatives, and coworkers – how are you being perceived now?

PERSON	PERCEPTION
1.	
2.	
3.	
4.	
5.	
6.	
7.	
8.	
9.	
10.	

Is your brand healthy?

Maintaining awareness of how you are being perceived and getting back value, in whatever form you decide that to be, should be monitored. I suggest you evaluate yourself quarterly. Keeping your brand word and your goals in mind, review the items you previously analyzed in the brand pulse exercise:

· Ask 5 people how they perceive you.
· Search your name and/or business name via Google and other search engines.
· Look at all of your social media accounts for consistency.
· Does your current business portrait and profile picture represent what you look like today?
· Review what others have posted about you online.
· Review written communications. If you posted an online blog or article, look at the comments.
· Review any audio recordings.
· Look at your wardrobe choices. Does anything need to be updated or changed?
· Have any of your personal or professional goals changed?
· Have you formed any new relationships?
· Are there any friends or acquaintances that may be damaging your brand?
· What are your daily habits and are they helping you get the results you want?

Rate the health of your brand using the scale below:

A – My brand is alive and well. I am in tip-top shape.

B – Doing great, but with a few tweaks I will be
   in tip-top shape.

C – Things are okay, but I could be doing much better.

D – Not what I expected, but I am ready to move up.

F – I have a lot of work to do as nothing is in line with
   what I want to portray.

If you are not happy with how you are being seen or perceived, change the view. That's what this entire book is about, to teach you how to change how people view you. But in doing this, there must be things you will not compromise. We all need to remember we will not relate to everyone, but we need to relate to those people who matter in our lives and those we wish to serve.

Finish this sentence: "I will never compromise..."

_____

_____

_____

_____

_____

The 5 things that are most important to me:

• _____

• _____

• _____

• _____

• _____

When people think of me, I want them to think of...

_____

_____

_____

_____

_____

Congratulations! You have defined yourself. You now have a clear understanding of who you are and the value you desire to bring forth to others. You are on your way to creating a personal brand with purpose.

Summary of I in I.C.U.

Being intentional establishes a mindset of deliberateness. It creates the framework to begin building out your personal brand. When well thought out, it becomes more of a strategy than left to chance. Without an intentional strategy, you run the risk of others defining you in a way that is likely not accurate. Being intentional gives you control and puts you in the driver's seat of how people will experience you. Being intentional will help you be consistent.

SECTION II
C – Consistent

"

con·sist·ent
adjective: free from variation
or contradiction

YOUR IMAGE NEVER SLEEPS.
IT IS ON 24/7.

"We become what we want
to be by consistently being
what we want to
become each day."
— Richard G. Scott

After you have gained clarity in the analysis phase, **the next step is to focus on presenting yourself across every channel in a consistent and intentional way.** The C stage of the process is where you focus on executing your personal style and image through disciplined consistency. **The C, or Consistency phase**, is important in building a signature brand because people come to expect the way we show up.

As mentioned in the introduction, people make an almost instant judgment of who you are within mere seconds.

Even before you speak a word or before you are introduced. Everything about you is judged from the very obvious aspects of your appearance, both in person and online, to the not so obvious aspects such as how you carry your body and the words you speak and write. Every aspect of you is a part of your brand. You can't play hooky with your personal brand and image. Just like in school, absences equate to a fail.

Through my experience – over 20 years, in fact – as a brand manager for one of the largest workers' compensation insurance companies in the Upper Midwest, I have learned by trial and error what enables a brand to have sticking power. Top of mind is always consistency. **Did we always nail it? No.** Will you always nail it? No, probably not. When you find yourself struggling or lacking visibility, be sure to do another BP check that you learned in the Intentional phase to determine if you are showing up consistently. I recommend you do these quarterly.

Consistency is vital to any brand, both corporate and personal. The overall goal in both is to have a synonymous

Consistency is vital to any brand, both corporate and personal.

message that is never left open to interpretation. By being consistent in every aspect, you teach people what they can expect from you. You teach them how to have a relationship with you. By doing so, you will deliver the value and results they expect from you. What they see is what they get. It keeps you top of mind when others need someone in your field.

26

While you do not always have control over a corporate brand, you do have complete control over your personal brand.

Your brand word pumps life into your personal brand.

A well thought-out brand will attract the right people to you and ensure you dominate in the space you want to own.

Think back to the word you chose that you want to own in the minds of others when they think of you.

My brand word is:

_____

You will now use this brand word to build your personal brand in how you look and in every touch point you have with others, whether the touchpoint is via an email communication, presenting in front of a group, posting online, or right down to how your office and home look. **All of these components work together to create a consistent flow of who you are.** It is like the blood flow in your body. Your blood travels everywhere throughout your body and is vital to each organ to make it function properly, ensuring all your body parts work together. Your personal brand is the same way. Each component must flow together, and into every aspect of who you are, in order to ensure you are living and breathing your brand in a consistent way.

Not only will you keep your brand word and overall goal in mind, you will also take your strengths and values into consideration as you build out who you are. These all come together to form you.

POP Your Brand

How do you make your personal brand POP? I believe there are three spaces we live out our personal brand.

They are:
1) the Personal space
2) the Online space
3) the Public space

This forms the acronym: POP. As you go about connecting your brand into each space, keep in mind it has to POP. It doesn't matter how great you are in one area, you have to be equally as great in the other two in order to be visible.

On a daily basis, we are involved in a variety of experiences in each of these spaces, sometimes simultaneously. Individually and collectively they nourish and reflect our brand. As we spend time in each space, we build up who we are. As you move about from space to space, pay attention to the influences in each and be acutely aware of your intentions and purpose.

In 2008 I was in Colorado Springs, CO, for a service club convention. The service club is called Cosmopolitan International and focuses on raising money for diabetes education and research. During my time in Colorado Springs, I had the opportunity to tour the United States Olympic Training Center. Seeing the athletes in action really is incredible. I greatly admire their discipline and focus. They are there for one reason and one reason only, to win. As I entered one of the gyms, I noticed a phrase painted boldly on a wall. The sign read, **"If you are going to be in the gym,** be in the gym." I have never forgotten this. The lesson is: whichever space you are in, be present.

Here is how I define these spaces and what is included in each:

Personal Space

This is who you are internally and externally. Personal space includes your physical self. It also includes those people that surround you like your family and friends. Your mother was right in that you become like the people you hang out with. They influence you and become a reflection of your choices. It also includes the personal spaces you occupy such as what home you live in, how your desk is organized, and even what vehicle(s) you own and drive.

- Physical Appearance
- Personal Style
- Body Language
- Verbal Communication
- Written Communication
- Family and Friends
- Desk and Office Space
- Home
- Vehicle

Online Space

Everything and anything that can be found about you online, whether you put it there or not.

- Social Media Profiles and Posts
- Blog Posts
- Online Articles
- Media Segments
- Personal or Business Website
- Images Associated with You via Search Engines
- Connections

Public Space

Your outward presence that people come in contact with when they meet or interact with you in your work or community. This will come into play more when we explore Section III – the U Section.

- Your Work or Business
- Business Partners and Coworkers
- Industry Organizations
- Network
- Clubs and Organizations
- Boards
- Volunteering
- Community Causes
- Local Events

Now let's take a further look into a few of the items from each. I did not categorize these under a specific space because there are times when it applies to more than one space.

Your appearance is your logo.

This is where your uniqueness comes to life. I like to compare your appearance to the **development of a company logo.** In the Intentional phase you have already defined what you as a brand stand for. The next step is to give the brand a distinct look. In corporate branding, a brand is first reflected via a logo. Similarly, in personal branding, your appearance is your logo.

In logo design, there may be a tendency to use a cheap online site or a friend who may have some creative background to design a logo. You will most certainly get a few logo options that you like, but I strongly believe this is not the place to be fast and cheap not only in logo design, but also in your personal presence. You are worth more than something created fast and cheap.

Be intentional in your appearance and be consistent.

The Image Language™

If you look up the word language in the Merriam-Webster dictionary, it is defined as, "a systematic means of communicating ideas or feelings by the use of conventionalized signs, sounds, gestures, or marks having understood meanings."

All elements of each language – visual, body, spoken, and written – act together as a single unit to create what I call **The Image Language™.**

Visual Language

Humans are wired to interpret things visually first. Visual language is a systematic means of communicating a message by using visual elements. This term was introduced by Robert E. Horn, an American political scientist who taught at Harvard, Columbia, and Sheffield Universities, and a visiting scholar at Stanford University's Center for the Study of Language and Information.

Think about this. **When you are posed with a question, often times you visually start to access pictures in your mind to help you answer the question.** Whether you are creating the picture in your mind or recalling one, you are using a visual to help you come up with an answer. The next time you ask people a question, watch the eyes. If you see the eyes move to the upper right, you will know they are accessing a visual element.

31

So, how does this relate to your personal brand? As mentioned previously, we think in pictures. So it matters how you present yourself visually. **One of the ways people will recall an interaction with us is how we appear visually.** We all have our own visual language. This is made up of how we look and what colors we wear. Two of the best ways to communicate who you are visually is by creating a signature look and utilizing color's message.

Create a Signature Look

There are many famous people – celebrities to politicians –who have created a distinct look that has become their signature. Whether the look of distinction was done with the feeling of an overall outfit or whether the person used a single accessory or color, **rest assured the complete look was done intentionally and consistently.** They defined their goal for what they wanted to be known for and knew what message they wanted to send by their visual appearance. Their goal guided their decision.

> I believe an item should have to earn a spot in your wardrobe.

I believe an item should have to earn a spot in your wardrobe. Ideally you need to be intentional and consistent on what you select to adorn yourself with.

If you look like you care about yourself, that translates into others knowing you will also take care of them. Being put together in an intentional and consistent way sends a strong message that you know who you are and what value you bring to others. This is a reflection of how you value yourself.

Your overall appearance must always be unique to you. **Do not look around to see what everybody else is doing or wearing.** This is where your brand word and the goals you defined for yourself come into play again, as well as your strengths and values. The look you select must be in alignment with your message. For example, if you want to be perceived as cutting edge, then your visual appearance must support this.

The first place to start is to create a signature look.
Here are some ways you can create your signature look in addition to dressing in a certain style and manner.

Necktie/Bow Tie
Select a necktie or bow tie in a particular color, pattern, or brand you like. A signature can be simply always wearing one.

Wrist Wear
Maybe you are person who has an affinity to wrist wear. Create a collection that people start to take notice of. You may find others start to compliment you on your timepieces.

Hairstyle
This one can be a bit tricky as hairstyles change so often, but a signature look can be created by consistently having some aspects stay the same. Think about the singer Cher, whose super long, black, straight hair was the envy of so many. An interesting point to note in high end fashion

shows is that most editors first look at a model's hair and then shoes to help them get a feel for what message the clothing designer is trying to tell.

Shoes
Examples include wearing sneakers with a business suit or always being in a red shoe.

Jewelry
Your look can be supported by always wearing something like a strand of pearls. Former First Lady of the United States, Barbara Bush, was rarely spotted without her signature strand of large pearls.

Hats
There are just some people we rarely see without a hat on. This can range from a simple fedora to a cowboy hat you might wear on a daily basis or a variety of extravagant hats to match outfits.

Handbag/Briefcase
Select a specific style, color, or brand. Your choice of bag says something about your personality.

Eyewear
This is one of my signature styles. I love eyewear and like to have fun with it. Choosing a specific shape, material, or color can do this. A signature look can even be that you create a collection of eyewear.

Nail Polish
Select a certain color or nail shape.

Jacket

Wear a jacket with almost every outfit. If you choose to do this, I encourage you to get them custom made where you can select the lining and thread color and other details to make the piece unique to you.

Jeans

You might choose to wear jeans for most occasions. If you do this, you need to be mindful in how you dress them up or down for specific occasions. Fit and color play an important role.

Scarves

Especially for women, this is an added piece that most do not take advantage of, so in that sense, a scarf can make you stand out. Scarves add a sense of elegance and give the message that you are detailed. Because it's the little detail, like a scarf, that you took the time to put on in an intentional way.

Makeup

A great way to do this is to select a specific lip color.

Socks

Especially for men, creative or fancy socks are a way you can add a bit of personality to your look.

Fragrance

Choose a perfume or cologne that evokes your inner essence.

Color

Similarly with a company logo, color plays an important role in communicating a message consistent with the overall brand. There is a language spoken by color. The colors you choose in your clothing can either increase or decrease your image. They can make you look credible, trustworthy, and powerful. They can make you stand out or blend in. They can help you persuade a person to your point of view, get this person to open up to you, and can even aid in getting you that promotion when you talk to your boss about a raise or stepping into a leadership position. Color plays a major role in the form of non-verbal communication. Color influences our emotions and behavior.

There is a language spoken by color

I am not going to go into major detail on this and it is touched upon again in the business portrait section. What is important to note is that **we all have colors that we look best in** and ones that help us deliver the message that is individual to us. Color supports your message and triggers the response you desire. A skilled personal brand expert or image consultant can help you choose the colors that bring forth your brand. Also worth mentioning is that there are cultural differences in how color is perceived and color's symbolism. I urge you to research this if you travel internationally.

Headshot

If I Googled all your social media accounts, what profile picture will I find of you? Is your profile picture a selfie or a professional portrait? Is the photo current or one from five years ago? If you want to be taken seriously in the business world, it is vital your profile picture and your business portrait reflect the true essence of who you are and what you look like today. In today's world, our first impression of people is often what we discover about them on the internet. This is one aspect of your image you need to be aware of and one that you can control by always being mindful of what you post as your profile picture.

The first thing we look for when we search for people online is what they look like. Can I find a picture of them? Simply by looking at a photograph of a person, we make judgments about him or her. We think to ourselves, is this a person I may like to work with? Do they look like they have the knowledge they say they do? Is this what I expect a person in this career to look like?

What you won't find me doing is taking a selfie that I use for my professional headshot. And what I also won't do is compromise the quality of my brand, both from a corporate branding and a personal branding perspective, with a low-quality headshot photo. I am much better than that. I am much better than a selfie, and so are you.

Just like in logo design, this is not the place to be fast and cheap. I recommend using a professional headshot photographer for your business portrait versus having your friend snap a photo with their cell phone. The quality speaks to how you perceive yourself. It is worth it to you to hire a professional photographer. The real value isn't in the money you spend. Actually, you aren't spending money. You are investing money, and the best place to invest is in yourself. It's proven that if you are willing to invest in yourself, others will be willing to invest in you.

I collaborated with professional photographer Chad Phillips, owner of **Chad Phillips Photography** in Sioux Falls, SD, to come up with some tips on what makes a great business portrait.

Seek out a professional portrait photographer
There really is an art to creating a quality business portrait. "We factor in what type of background you want. What is the best lighting? Should your portrait be in studio, on location, or in your office?" notes Chad.

Think about the brand word you chose for yourself
Most photographers will ask you what you want to portray through your photographs. This is where you can communicate with them your brand. The goal is to not have your headshot look like everyone else's. You need one that makes you memorable. Your portrait must not lack individuality. Everyone should have a distinct look and their personality should come through in their headshot.

Consider where your portrait will be used

"We work with many business professionals. How you market to your clients may be different than how you want to appear within other professional circles. We typically will create two different images for our clients: one that is inviting, approachable, and caters to the general public with a neutral background. The second image can be a different outfit, maybe a suit and more of a business background."

Wear long sleeves or a jacket

Many people are conscious of their arms. Covering them helps to bring the focus to your face and smile. If you are in a professional field, long sleeves are viewed as more formal and businesslike. The more flesh one sees, the more casual an overall look becomes. The only exception to this is in eveningwear.

Wear clothing that fits closely to the body

This helps show your shape and avoids adding extra weight to your photograph. We always hear the camera adds 10 pounds. That truly depends on the lighting and the skill of the photographer. However, you can help ensure you look your slimmest by wearing clothes that show your silhouette.

Solid fabrics work best

Avoid wrinkled or bulky fabrics. Any little wrinkle is magnified on camera. Anything bulky adds weight. Trendy clothes can look dated quickly. Too much pattern can have a strobing effect on camera. It is best to choose classic styles, but again, you can add a bit of your personality to classic pieces.

Color plays a role in how others perceive you

Think about what image you want to portray. Color plays a role in how others perceive you. For example, **blue is always a great choice for business.** Blue is reliable and constant. The darker the blue, the more powerful the color. **Red indicates power and is stimulating since it immediately increases blood pressure when you look at it.** If you feel like you are lacking power, put on red. **Purple is considered elegant and creative.** Purple combines the power of red with the calmness of blue. **Brown has the connotation of being wholesome and supportive.** Darker and mid-tone colors work best on camera. And do not be afraid to add some personality with a punch of color by **adding a great pocket square, necktie, or scarf.**

Little to no jewelry works best

Jewelry can pick up shine and reflects light back to the camera lens. It can also be distracting in a picture. We don't want the focus to go to the jewelry. We want the focus to go to your face.

Get your haircut a few days before your session

Don't wait until the day of your photo session.

Try to relax

Chad adds, "We never rush into a portrait. We take time to get to know our clients and build a relationship. Your true smile comes out when you are relaxed."

These are just a few tips to get you on your way to putting

your best face forward. A good portrait will bring to life your personality and your personal brand.

Desk and Home
You can tell a lot about peoples' personalities and values by what they surround themselves with in their homes and in their offices. What you put on display tells others what you want them to take notice of. In fact, if you are having trouble figuring out your personal style, take a look around your home. Typically people decorate their homes in a taste that is similar to their personal style preference. For example, if you tend to lean more towards a very traditional style, this translates to being traditional in your clothing choices and your beliefs.

"Behavior is the mirror in which everyone shows their image." – Johann Wolfgang von Goethe

Body Language
There are numerous books written on body language. While I do not pretend to be a body language expert, of one thing I am certain: how you physically carry yourself speaks to how you think of yourself.

When I was 39, I enrolled in modeling school. You might ask yourself, why in the world would anyone at that age want to enroll in modeling school? **Here is why: I needed to learn to carry and conduct myself in a powerful way.** I spent countless hours on a runway learning to walk gracefully in high heels and how to use posture as a way to present myself in a powerful and professional way. I used to slump my shoulders, which diminishes your power. I remember clearly the first time the instructor taught my class on what your posture really should be. She told us to put our hands on our hips bending the elbows back at bit towards the middle of the back. Then, keeping your shoulders in that place, drop your arms along side your body. That's where your shoulders should be. This posture felt awkward, but I learned over time to carry my body in this manner. Having great posture reflects an attitude of confidence and commands a presence.

Spoken and Written Language

...there are other aspects such as tone of voice and pace that play into the perception others form of you.

How you speak or write and your word choices play a part in how you are perceived by others. If you are by nature a witty person, then the words you speak and write should reflect your wittiness. If you think of yourself as thoughtful, the words you say or write to others need to be thoughtful in every sense. **If you want to come across as powerful, then you should avoid using slang or improper grammar.** It's really quite this simple.

With the spoken word, there are other aspects such as tone of voice and pace that play into the perception others form of you. Not only from the perspective of you speaking to people face-to-face, but this is also important in voicemail. If I call your phone and get your voicemail, what does your message say and what impression does it give? If you leave me a voicemail, what impression about you as a person should I get from listening to your message? Again, this all ties back to your brand word and your goals.

 With the written word, more thought needs to go into your word choices since people will only be reading your words. We all risk the chance our written word can be misunderstood and taken in the wrong way. When we don't have sound attached to the words, some translation gets lost. Be very careful when you are writing any type of correspondence or online post, even down to how you sign off on an email, that the words you choose and the overall tone of them combined gives the impression you want and is in alignment with how you are presenting yourself overall. Again, consistency matters.

Communication Tips

· Avoid filler words: "like," "um," "so."
 These words sound unprofessional and unpolished. You sound unsure of yourself. Know that it is okay to pause while thinking of what you want to say versus filling the silence with "um."

· Repeat a person's name when talking to them.
 We all like to hear our own name.

· If you have to deliver bad news, try to communicate with individuals in person. Written communication doesn't allow you to soften difficult messages with nonverbal cues, nor does this allow you to deal immediately with intense emotion.

· Show genuine interest when listening to a person speak.
I like to say, "be where you are."

· Make sure you record your voicemail instead of using
a canned one and pay attention to the tone of your voice.
No one wants to be greeted by a cold voicemail.

Online

Our world today is submerged in living out much of our
life online. In many ways it has leveled the playing field. We
find ourselves continuously hitting the scroll button until
something stands out and makes us stop and click to learn
more. We quickly look through an online site and decide
almost instantly if we want to engage deeper. You have
to show up in a way that makes people want to open the
door to who you are and what you offer.

You must be memorable.

People can hide behind a well built-out online presence.
That is why it is so vital that you are consistent in how you
present yourself in each space: personally, online, and
publicly. If any one of these is not consistent with the
other two, it diminishes credibility and trust, which are at
the forefront of every relationship whether it is personally
or professionally.

A LinkedIn Profile That Stands Out

In many ways, LinkedIn is the new resume or CV. LinkedIn is the go-to place to find out more about a person's expertise, how they position themselves in their space, and gain insight on what it is like to work with them via testimonials. In fact, if you have to pick just one place to start strengthening your personal brand, I recommend you start with LinkedIn. Here are 5 tips to help you stand out, or as I like to say, **"make you strategically visible."**

PROFESSIONAL HEADSHOT AND BACKGROUND PHOTO. LinkedIn is a professional social media platform. That alone calls for a professional headshot. Your photo is by far the most important element and makes that first impression of you. People do a search online for you before they meet you. You want to make sure you have a professional photo versus a low quality image. A quality photo gives the sense you are serious about who you are and your career goals. **I'm not saying the photo has to be stoic; it can have some personality.** Just make sure the overall image represents who you are and what you stand for. Also, most people don't take advantage of customizing the background photo. You can use this space to increase brand awareness.

HEADLINE. This appears beside your name any time you post or comment. This is valuable real estate! Don't just put your title, but **describe how you help people and think about what keywords people will use to search for your expertise.** Showcase what you do.

45

PROFILE SUMMARY. This can be daunting to fill out, but think of the profile summary in terms of how you can help people and what problems you solve. This doesn't have to be long, but please fill this out.

CUSTOMIZE YOUR OWN LINKEDIN PROFILE URL. Which one looks better: 1) www.linked.com/in/XFOE32 or 2) www.linkedin.com/in/sheilamooreanderson? Yes, #2 looks better and more professional. A custom URL is also a way to brand your name.

ASK FOR RECOMMENDATIONS. This is a place where others can do the bragging for you. People want to know what it's like to work with you. If you feel uncomfortable asking, start by completing a recommendation for one of your contacts on LinkedIn. They will greatly appreciate having a recommendation and will likely reciprocate. Strive to get 10 of them.

Doing these 5 things help you elevate your LinkedIn profile in a crowded space.

Create a Personal Brand Board
As in corporate branding, brand boards are designed to guide you as you continue to build your brand. They serve as a reference to keep you on track. Here are the elements for a Personal Brand Board. Simply write down all the elements of your brand that you have identified. You can do this on your computer and keep the brand board handy to monitor yourself.

YOU

Personal Name
Do you want to use your full name or middle initial?

Your Brand Word

Other Word Descriptors
These come from when you narrowed down the words you want to be known by to three words.

Values

Strengths

Personal Brand Statement or Elevator Pitch
If you have mantra or have created a statement about who you are, be sure to capture that.

Title(s)

STYLE

Signature Style
Write out what key elements make up your personal style.

Color Palette
What colors are you going to wear? This also includes what colors you will use in various marketing pieces you may design for yourself.

IMAGERY
Business Portrait(s)
Insert your business portrait.

Imagery Inspiration – Insert images, photos, or illustrations that evoke your brand. You may not use them in anything, but they give you an overall feeling for what your brand stands for. For example, if your personal brand is cutting edge, then you might include a black sports car.

ELEMENTS

Typography
What fonts will you use for various purposes?

Logo.

ONLINE PRESENCE

Social Media Handles
List out all your handles.

Social Media Covers
Insert what all of your social media covers look like.

Blog Post Template
Insert a picture or descriptor of what your blog post looks like. This includes layout, fonts, color, and tone of voice you will use.

Website URL

STATIONERY

Business Card Template

Insert a picture of your business card.

Newsletter Template

Insert a picture or descriptor of what your newsletter looks like. This includes layout, fonts, color, and tone of voice you will use.

Personalized Stationery

If you have had notecards or personalized stationery designed, insert a picture of the final product. If you don't have anything yet, insert pictures of ideas you like.

VOICE

Voicemail Message Script

Write out your voicemail script.

Email/Letter Complimentary Close

Decide on a consistent complimentary close you will use. List the closing here.

Email Signature

Decide on a consistent email signature you will use. Insert the email signature here.

Writing Style

Define your writing style. You can simply use a few words to describe your overall writing style.

OTHER

Trademarks.

List any trademarks you may have.

ADD MISCELLANEOUS DETAILS AS NEEDED

Summary of C in I.C.U.

Being consistent eliminates confusion. Consistency sets an expectation that is reinforced with each interaction. Being consistent shows your **deliberate focus** in delivering the experience of you in a way others will come to expect from only you. This creates trust and sends the message you are dependable. When you are consistent, you become recognizable, thus reinforcing your message. When others are faced with a choice between you or someone else, the ability to remember you will be an advantage.

SECTION III
U – You

"

you
pronoun: anyone at all

DOES YOUR PRESENCE
MAKE AN IMPACT?

If your presence doesn't make an impact, your absence won't make a difference.

66 I.C.U. really simplified my life so I can concentrate on being present with my friends, employees, and clients."
Jason Player,
CIO/CMO and Headshot Photographer

After you have looked inward and defined who you are and consistently execute your authentic style elements into the spaces of your life, the last phase of I.C.U. is "You."
The U step is two-fold. First, it represents authenticity. You must be you in every way at all times. Conforming to societal pressures or influences may, at times, seem to be the easy path to take. It may even feel good for awhile. In the long run, it is not the easiest path and will cause confusion

not only internally, but externally in how others view you. Being inauthentic runs the risk of you not performing at your optimum level. It can be a risk to be yourself, but it is even riskier to be something you are not. You will only be truly happy and bring value to others when you are yourself.

No one else has your strengths, values, aspirations, views, demeanor, compassion, personality, voice, or appearance.

No one else has everything you have. No one else has your strengths, values, aspirations, views, demeanor, compassion, personality, voice, or appearance. Quite simply, no one else can be you except you. Recognize the value your difference brings.

Second, the U step is about solidifying the brand experience by prioritizing "you" or relationships, audiences, and communities.

Going through the I.C.U. process develops who you are as a person and the value you provide to others. Because in the end, personal branding isn't all about you, it's about what you bring to others.

Remember in the intentional phase you were asked **what word you want to own in the mind of others**. That is the end game. The goal of personal branding is to own your brand word in everything you do. You want every experience with you to connect back to your brand word and your goals. It defines the value you bring to others. Once you know who you are and the value you bring to others, you can simply take your focus off yourself and begin to focus on adding into the lives of others.

Leaders know the focus isn't on them. **The focus is about helping and inspiring their team to move or act on a shared vision.** The same holds true in personal branding. You now know who you are and are able to go out into any space, such as your community, and bring value to every area you are in. You will bring with you an experience that is unique to you. You will bring with you an unrivaled set of differentiators that no one else has. You will know what strengths you bring to the table that will help others and have an impact that no one else can have. As the saying goes, "no one is you and that is your power."

Let's take a look at some ways you can bring forward your value to others while continuing to build out your personal brand in public spaces.

Public Space
The following offer ways in how you can gain visibility and give value in your community or industry:

- Volunteer for a fundraiser
- Join a corporate or community board
- Join a service club
- **Be a guest speaker at an industry event**
- Run for public office
- **Be a guest on a local radio show**
- Be a guest on a local TV station
- Write a guest column in a publication
- Lead a meeting
- Start a blog

57

• Join groups online, such as on LinkedIn, and share your expert thoughts in the group

5 Ways Volunteering Builds Your Personal Brand

It is absolutely true that we are all busier than we used to be. There are many things vying for our attention – from kids and family to our business commitments. In fact, many times all these commitments feel down right exhausting.

And you are thinking to yourself right this very moment, "so now you are telling me to carve out time to volunteer?"

The number one excuse I hear all of the time when I advise people to get involved in their community by volunteering at events or joining a nonprofit board or a service club is "I don't have time." As with anything in life, the benefits of how you spend your time must be worth the investment. Because there are two things the world doesn't make more of and that is **land and time.**

Volunteering was not something I grew up doing much of, nor did I see members of my family giving back in the community by volunteering. Sure there were the occasional baseball games of my brother's where we had to work the concession stand, but that was basically it. Other than a few instances like this, I wasn't exposed to much volunteering. So when I decided to join a service club in 1995, I was not only busy in both my personal and business lives, but I was about to embark on something that was, quite frankly, way out of my comfort zone. And that's exactly why I joined. You see I used to be very shy. I was uncomfortable being in a room full of people I did not know. What would I say to them? How did I go about starting a conversation with people I knew nothing about? Having to talk to people I did not know was paralyzing. Those that know me well always find this fact a bit unbelievable. But that's the whole point. Being involved with a service club helped me overcome shyness and increase my self-esteem. It was the number one way I was able to grow personally and professionally.

> # Having to talk to people I did not know was paralyzing.

Here are five ways volunteering can help you build your personal brand:

1. Enhance Skills

Volunteering can help with many aspects of sharpening your skills or discovering a hidden talent. There might be instances when you will take the lead on a project or lead a committee or board. I do not care how great of a leader anyone is, managing a nonprofit board is always a personal growth opportunity. Besides honing people skills, other skills you may learn include developing a strategic plan, preparing a budget, learning to fundraise, mastering decision making, or marketing an event.

The more unique skills you have, the more you differentiate yourself.

2. Improve Speaking

It may be as simple as learning not to be afraid to speak up with your ideas in a small group setting, or it may be as big as being the president of a service club and having to regularly speak to a room full of members. There are opportunities at both ends of the spectrum. For the most part, we are all comfortable talking about what we know very well, but when the time comes to speaking about something new to us, this provides an opportunity for growth. As mentioned earlier, I was extremely shy and the thought of standing up in front of others was not something I saw myself doing. **Now with over 20 years of volunteer and nonprofit board experience – which included serving as the International President for a service club – I have overcome this to the point that I do keynote speeches.** If I can do it, you certainly can!

3. Build Confidence

Building confidence goes hand-in-hand with learning new skills and becoming more comfortable speaking in front of others. Your confidence will grow when you become better at anything you do.

4. Develop Empathy

Empathy is about putting the needs of others before your own. That is absolutely what you do when you volunteer. Giving back demonstrates you care and that you are able to be sensitive to the needs of others. This teaches you to nurture relationships and take your eyes off of yourself. Volunteering allows you to be open to different views and gain real connections with people, which builds trust. Trust is at the core of every successful business and personal interaction.

5. Gain Visibility

When you put yourself out in the community, you will meet new people, thus strengthening your network. Many movers and shakers in your field or community are already volunteering and looking to connect with others. Building relationships is vital to anyone's success. You may gain new clients or being visible in the community may lead to new career opportunities. The more you are seen, the more people will think about you for various business, or even personal, interactions.

Building your personal brand by giving back to your community is a powerful win-win. These five areas develop who you are as a person and the value you provide to others. Because in the end, personal branding is about what you bring to others.

Work Space

Assets are critical to a company's success with their purpose being to increase the value of the organization. So how else can you add value to your organization without dipping into the bottom line?

The answer: Personal Branding.

Companies spend thousands of dollars on corporate branding elements such as logo, website, and marketing collateral, but many overlook the fact that every employee is a branding asset. When one thinks of gauging value back from what they put into something, they typically think in terms of ROI. Instead of a return on investment, think of ROI in terms of Return on Image®. An employee's personal brand creates real value. A personal brand can elevate individuals to meet their goals and the goals of the company, while also growing influence for both. Influence is power, which, in turn, cultivates trust and builds your reputation as a leader in your space. It's been said over and over that people do business with people, not companies.

Here are five ways employees can influence a corporate brand while building their personal brand:

1. Create Content

This is vital (my definition of vital: without it you die) in establishing expertise. Creating content is the first place one should start in developing their personal brand. Companies need to encourage employees to blog, be guest editors in publications, or even publish case studies that are relevant to the company's market. Let their personality come through in their writings. The company should then leverage that content every chance they get such as reposting portions of the content as social media posts. Having them create content helps establish them, and the company, as a leader or expert in their field. **People want to hire authorities.**

2. Speaking Events

In today's world we are so connected, that we are, at times, starving for human connection. This is a great way to humanize a brand. Employees can be guest speakers at associations, clubs, industry events, or be a guest on a podcast. If possible, employees should get photos of them speaking or better yet, get their appearance recorded on video, and, again, leverage these talks as much as possible.

3. Community Involvement

A great place to be seen is in our own communities sharing our gifts and kindness with others. Companies should consider paying for employees to join a service club or be on a non-profit board. They may even take on leadership roles within these organizations, which helps build both their personal brand and the corporate brand.

4. LinkedIn Profile

This was covered previously but is worth noting again. We all know LinkedIn is a place to grow connections and attract new business clients. LinkedIn is one of the first places we all go to find out about each other. We look at a person's accomplishments, what others say about working with them, and how they can add value. In fact, we tend to go there before we have any human interaction with each other. First of all, we want to know what a person looks like. A profile picture can have some personality, but remember this is a professional site, after all. After we look at the photo, we want to know their title. In fact, here is where you can be creative. Your title does not have to be your actual title, but rather how you help others. This appears by the photo every time a person posts, so the title is a very important element. Be sure your company or the company you work for has a LinkedIn page that employees can connect to.

5. Company Website

The second most visited page on most websites is the **About Us** page. Here is where companies can showcase their staff with a bio and links to their personal social media sites as well as listing any published content or videos they have created. **The purpose is for visitors to have no doubt in their minds that the company employs the best.**

There is a lot of noise out there. We are all fighting to be seen. By incorporating the steps above, both the company and you can gain strategic visibility through personal branding.

All of the above makes you visible as a leader in the public space. As you continue to add value to others, you will continue to build your personal brand.

Summary of U in I.C.U.

Having permission to be you has always been there. My guess is that you have known this for quite some time. You just needed to have a little reminder. **The ability to go into the world and bring your value to others in your community and in your work is a gift unique to you.** You have peace in knowing exactly who are you and can focus on being present wherever you are and in every moment. There are no distractions.

I.C.U. IN ACTION

CEO develops personal brand to support growth and complement his corporate brand.

"As a CEO, sometimes I forget that I am an extension of my company's brand. Sheila Anderson took me full circle discussing my goals and helping me make a plan to reach them. She coached me through a transformation that helped me discover my personal brand - one that complements my company's brand, allows me to be me, and is helping move my company toward even more success!"

Michael Winkleman
CEO
PatientX

CLIENT PROFILE
Michael Winkleman is the CEO of PatientX. PatientX is a trusted partner and leader in healthcare marketing.

THE SITUATION
Michael was in the beginning process of developing the brand for PatientX. He approached Sheila to help him become visible in the marketplace as a thought leader.

THE PROCESS AND SOLUTION

Michael was focused on building the company brand. He was absorbed with the typicals such as the culture of the business, colors, fonts, imagery, what the office was going to look like, and just really how they were going to set themselves apart in the marketplace. What Michael started to realize was that since the company specialized in the healthcare industry there was not a lot of marketing or advertising companies that really stood out differently. They really held true to the culture of corporate environment or being very careful with the messaging they had for the different facilities and still trying to be creative. This lead Michael to focus on a brand that was very vibrant and colorful and that also had a message that was loud and clear.

"I was really happy with the image and brand of the company and how it was coming together, but now I thought to myself here I am, the new business development for my company, what do I do? How am I going to get out there?"

Michael knew he needed to become a thought leader in the space of healthcare because his ideas and approach to healthcare marketing are different. He wanted to take that information he was learning through implementing big data, social data, and think data and do speaking engagements. His initial thought to be seen as a thought leader and to gain visibility was to start speaking. This is when he approached Sheila for help.

I.C.U. IN ACTION

INTENTIONAL

Sheila asked Michael a series of questions ranging from what his goals and strengths were to identifying his brand word.

"So that's when I sat down with Sheila. She said to me you have a great corporate brand. I love what is going on. It is really going to stand out, but how about you? What's your brand?"

CONSISTENT

Michael confessed even though he was in a creative field, when it came to his personal brand he was pretty blah. He typically wore a black shirt or a white shirt like everyone else in the crowd, but it never really energized him or brought forth his strengths and goals. Where he was trying to be different was in the contextual part. But found he couldn't stand out in the crowd and get that contextual part if he was not different. So he was not really trying to be different in that perspective.

Together Michael and Sheila identified key components Michael could implement to create a personal brand that was vibrant. Regarding personal style, they discussed the psychology of color and what colors identified best with the goals of Michael's personal brand. It was decided that red, gray, and blue would be become the core of his wardrobe. They created a signature style for Michael that incorporated red Adidas; red and blue suit jackets and red, blue, and gray shoes that match both the company brand and Michael's personal brand.

U

Michael's biggest takeaway: just be you. He gained confidence and clarity allowing him to bring forth his value to the marketplace that is unique to him. His inner essence is exuding through every touch point he has with others. His company also went through a rebrand that now ties his personal brand to the corporate brand.

The brands are now a unified message.

Final Thoughts

I love the phrase in business known as the **Thud Factor.** Essentially it means having weight. For example, when a person gives you a business card or a brochure, does it look and feel wimpy or does it give the impression a lot of work was put into creating it? Is there is a heft to how you feel about the card? When you drop the brochure on your desk, does it barely make a noise or does it make a thud? We judge things on how they look and feel.

I'd like to leave you with one final thought. I.C.U. is really all about your Thud Factor. I.C.U. helps you make a thud when you show up. I.C.U. makes you look and feel significant; you have put a lot of work into yourself, and you care enough about yourself to take the effort to be your best in every way. I.C.U. translates to others that you care enough to take care of yourself, and thus, you will take care of them in the same way.

I.C.U. guides you to building an intentional, consistent brand that impacts the people who are meaningful in your life. Using I.C.U., you become a constant example of your brand word, goals, values, and strengths. All the pieces of your personal brand come together into one picture making a statement that is distinctly yours. I.C.U. helps you cultivate and own what lives in the minds of others after they have interacted with you. **You become an experience connecting with a purpose – intentionally and consistently.**

You will have them at hello.

Please connect and share your I.C.U. experiences with me by posting on social media using the hashtag: #ICURule.

I am excited to see how I.C.U. impacts you
in a powerful way!

Sheila

ABOUT THE AUTHOR

 Sheila A. Anderson, CEO of **Image Power Play,** is not only a personal brand strategist and speaker, she is an image and impression management expert driven to empower corporate professionals across the globe in grow-ing their strategic visibility. Her exceptional talent benefits executives at any level in polishing **all facets of their brand – appearance, attire, behavior, body language and more – to power brand-aligned personal presence and commu-nication style.** Personally drawn to the influence of impres-sion management, Sheila has successfully cultivated her own unique style as a business owner, image consultant, personal brand strategist, and sought-after speaker. From professional modeling that includes runway, print, and TV commercial work to a career in brand management, Sheila draws from over two decades of experience when speaking

and producing in the world of impression management.

Sheila is a charter member of the **C-Suite Network Advisors™,** an elite group of the most trusted advisors to C-level executives. She is the author of the book ICU, Breathing Life Back into Your Personal Brand. Sheila owns the registered trademark **Return on Image®.** She is a member of the National Speakers Association.

Community-focused, Sheila is a member of Cosmopolitan International, a service club that raises money for diabetes education and research. **In 2013-2014, she proudly held the office as the organization's International President, being only the third woman since its inception in 1918 to hold this prestigious office.** Prior to this, she held the office as the Vice President of Marketing for three years. She served on the Cosmopolitan Diabetes Foundation Board in 2015 and 2016. She currently serves on the Adult Advisory Board for the non-profit, Simon Says Give.

Sheila was named first runner-up in the 2012 Mrs. South Dakota-America pageant and has mentored pageant contestants and served as a judge.

ABOUT IMAGE POWER PLAY

Image Power Play believes everyone is the Chief Experience Officer of his or her personal brand. Connecting with a purpose is always top of mind throughout the entire strategic process.

Image Power Play is an impression management and personal brand company dedicated to bringing forth intentional, consistent, and authentic interactions with others. The company is focused on creating influence through image. Sheila A. Anderson, CEO and Founder, works with emerging and established leaders, as well as companies, that put value on proper positioning and being strategically visible in the space they want to own.

Gaining a **Return on Image®** puts measurable value on the impact one's image has personally and professionally. Image Power Play's Return on Image® services create real value and elevate leaders to meet their goals and grow their influence. This is done by taking a strategic look at every aspect of a person's image – spanning from appearance and behavior to how one communicate both verbally and nonverbally to a social media strategy and community interactions.

Image Power Play designed **The I.C.U. Rule™,** a process to work with leaders to lean into personal style and authentic brand. Through an analysis phase, leaders focus in on being intentional before encounters occur. After gaining clarity in the analysis phase, the focus moves into executing personal style and image through disciplined consistency. Once leaders look inward and defined who they are and consistently execute authentic style elements into the spaces of their lives, the last phase of I.C.U. is you. The U step is really about solidifying the brand experience by prioritizing others (you) and relationships, audiences, and communities. These steps result in career advancement, increasing one's center of influence, and being recognized as a leader.

Image Power Play offers personal branding strategies through one-on-one coaching, corporate coaching, workshops, and keynote speeches.